Amitriptyline Queen

Jaden Christopher

chipmunkapublishing

the mental health publisher

All rights reserved, no part of this publication may be reproduced by any means, electronic, mechanical photocopying, documentary, film or in any other format without prior written permission of the publisher.

Published by

Chipmunkapublishing

PO Box 6872

Brentwood

Essex CM13 1ZT

United Kingdom

http://www.chipmunkapublishing.com

Copyright © Jaden Christopher 2011

ISBN   978-1-84991-631-8

Chipmunkapublishing gratefully acknowledge the support of Arts Council England.

Author Biography

Jaden Christopher was born in 1983 and is currently a Masters in Mental Health Counseling student. She was diagnosed with Bipolar I Disorder and Borderline Personality Disorder at the age of 18. Jaden has a history of poly substance abuse and is currently in recovery. She began writing at as a teenager and documenting her life in the form of poetry and letters. After nine years of scribbling in note pads she put her thoughts together in this book. Jaden contributes her recovery to self advocacy, self education, a strong support system of friends, psychopharmacology, and above all her mother.

Jaden Christopher

This book is dedicated to:

Ophelia 2003

Jaden Christopher

Slit Wrists and Forehead Kisses

With that kiss
You left me for dead
Made me slit my wrists
Infected my head

Cheater
Bastard
Whore

Is that who I slit them for?

Slit them for the illness
A martyr for the cause
The stigma shall not catch me
As I take this little pause
A small psychotic break
The whore I did forsake

Chronic
Persistent

I don't want that
I can't stop that
Your forehead kiss
Has made me sick.

No one wakes up and says, "Gee, I hope I have a mental illness when I grow up." Still, some of us get it, and the worst thing you can do is run from it. Acceptance is a key part of recovery. Learning to acknowledge it, educate yourself, and accept your limitations... no matter what they are, because your strengths will always outweigh them. Just like cancer, the sooner you catch it and deal with it, the easier it is to adjust.

One of the worst things is having to adjust your dreams. I always wanted to be a doctor. I wanted to work with HIV antibodies in a research lab. At age sixteen, I learned that a friend had HIV, and all I ever wanted to do was save his life. Now, I have to worry about saving my own. I had the grades to be a doctor in high school and carried a 3.8 GPA at Loyola University, Chicago, six months prior to my first psychotic break. I was a Pre-Med Biology Major, and I was going to make it. I dropped out of school after I found James asleep next to a naked Veronica, December 22nd 2001.

I had dated James from the 4th of August, 2001, after graduating high school as the National Honor Society President, Student Body Vice President, and Prom Queen. I was a varsity cheerleader, and always peppy, happy, and cheerful. Towards my senior year, things began to change. I noticed I was becoming more vengeful, especially surrounding the topics of my friend's relationships. I became hypersexual, had racing thoughts, never slept, but couldn't get to school on time. I was almost suspended and spoke with rapid, pressured speech.

Amitriptyline Queen

I attended a Catholic high school in a small town. My class was a close family of twenty-nine, and as an adult I deeply regret that we didn't stay as close as we were in high school. However, my best friends today, I have known since I was twelve. They have watched me undergo numerous medications, psychoanalysis, more mood swings than I can count, and have stood by me through the men, the drugs, and the suicide attempts.

I contribute parts of my recovery to my support system and these high school friends. After all, it was four of them who picked me up off the street the morning I had my first psychotic break, bandaged me up, made me watch stupid movies, took me out in major catatonic states and tried their damnedest to make me laugh. I don't know if they ever understood what had happened that day... but it involved knives, blood, beatings, and lots of crying. I don't remember much... but that's in part because I'm too scared.

My "genie in his S10 pickup" had stood by me through so much. On the 22nd of December, 2001, he sat with me at the mall while smoking pack after pack of cigarettes; wrapped up wrists, catatonic, and psychotic. And he came to take me home. Today, we are still best friends.

James and I were young. Everyone thought he 'did' this to me; no one understands that until afterwards. James didn't do anything to me that wouldn't have happened later in life. Mental illness is a ticking time bomb and you don't get to choose who hits the detonator.

Jaden Christopher

January 2001

Dear Doctor,

I remember the first time it happened. The first knife I used, the first numb wave that came over me, the first time I cleaned my cuts, and the first time I hide them from you; the first time I lied. I recall looking down at the white bandages and being in love with my tangible sadness. Those beautiful bloody scars that I picked at for weeks. Oh, that wonderful feeling of coming so close to dying… the heightened excitement of someone finding me in a pool of blood semi-conscious and dribbling the words 'help me'. The feelings that it would invoke in James; he'd surely leave Veronica then…

Doctor, I need some attention. I need some help. I need someone to notice how much I hurt. And I need James to notice how much he has hurt me. Look at what he's done; what he's made me do. I cannot express it in words. You ask me to show you my arms. Guilt. Embarrassment. Shame. Stop re-traumatizing me. Only James should see the cuts, he did this. He made me sick. Talk to him about what I've gone though, talk to him about what he did. Talk to him to fix me… make him talk to me, please doctor. Please bring him back to me.

Doctor, he's a bastard, she's a whore, he's a cheater… what am I, doctor? Am I sick? I am not going to the hospital. I am not a drug addict. I am not crazy. I am not a psycho. I'm not one of those people. I'm scared, lost, betrayed, lied to, cheated on, I have a reason. I'm not just crazy. I need your pills though.

Can someone talk to me? About what's wrong… why is everyone talking about me? Why not to me? What are you not telling me? Doctor, do you think I can't handle what you're telling my mom about me? Doctor, tell me, please, what's wrong with me…?

I will not be crazy, doctor, because then I will have no voice. I will not sign that power of attorney, doctor, because then I will have no choice. I will not go to your hospital, doctor, because then I will have no hope. Do not validate my psychosis. I'm terrified. Make it all stop. But please doctor; do not prescribe the death of a Prom Queen...

~Help me~

Jaden Christopher

Steel Reserved

Liquid steel drains into my stomach with that malt liquor
mask
Wear it to cover the abuser from my childhood
A flare up of demons equate the cold steel that whispers
a netting of scars across her wrists
I hide in the shadows of manhood, a reflection of my
pseudo-father

Steel plated walls lock me in a mould
Factory child from an unknown production line
I was passed and passed and store bought regretfully
Raised in the steel belt with factory cold emotions

Cold steel butcher
She thinly shaves pieces of me away
Cut through, it's up to you
How did you cut though my steel armor?
I am stunning E-coli under the light of your display case

Naked without steel reserve
Shiny silver to protect me from the blade
The cold steel she usually turns on herself
Black Widow eats me whole in my afterglow.

Lesbian Love Song

Straddled above me
She sat hard on my naked body
I stared into her eyes
Wide brown
Glazed over flat
Skin smacking
Hair pulling
Screaming

The room was spinning
Fire on her wrists
Stumbling
I Ran
Safety
Locked the bathroom door
Hot tears, vomit, and blood
My mouth began to swell
Aching
Reached for a towel
Something to cover me
Swiftly out the door

Please don't push me down these stairs.

Jaden Christopher

Aladdin's Castle

Surrounded by the neon lights of Aladdin's castle
Arose through the smoke from her Shield cigarettes
Her genie appeared in his red S10 pickup

Sturdy, with no words
Stoic pillar in the middle of nothing
Crumbling as she stared through me

Dry lips pursed, sucking one after another
20 down like liquid in this material desert
Inhaling the Cyanide that will give her what she wants

Meditative state to her God that no longer exists
Eyes bloodshot as if she was up all night praying
Chanting, holding her rosary, like an Old Catholic on her deathbed

An empty chair, rocking, isolated in a room
One lone curl bouncing across her face
Dancing a trance to music only she can hear

With an involuntary breath
She exhaled
Take me home.

February 2002

Dear James,

It's been two months; I don't know why I always get my hopes up that I will end up back with you. I mean I know it never works out, I know there isn't anything there. Yet, for some reason my heart just won't let you go, and it really does hurt so much. I am always in tears.

I have loved and lost, and trust me, it is better to have never loved at all. I wish I didn't know the feeling of abandonment, because it seems to be an emotion that can take over everything in me. I don't know how to accept defeat in this situation, I don't know how to give you up and let you go in my heart. My mind already knows you're gone. It's so hard to look at your picture, I can't stop myself from wanting to crawl into a little ball on your lap and lay with my head on your chest. It's the only comforting thing I have ever known. When we do talk, I can't handle it when you're mean or when we get into fights, because I get so mad, and I know if I say one wrong thing I could lose you forever. So I write…

It hurts to give so much love away and not feel any of it back. It hurts to not be able to kiss you whenever I want, or even at all. Mainly it hurts to not feel your arms around me when I sleep at night.

It's hard to know I have been replaced, and someone else is getting the love I have wanted to feel again for so long.

It's so sad that one day, I will have to accept the fact that if I want to live a normal life, if either one of us does, we can't do it together. I just can't control myself when it comes to you and that is so destructive. I set myself up for something I know doesn't exist, and I don't even know I am doing it until it's too late. I am forever breaking my own heart...

But that second I spend with my head against your chest and your arms around me is so worth it.

Even if it's only for a second...

~I love you~

Virginity

Pale white innocence, yet I am not scared

Catholic school girl virgin and yes, I know it's wrong

And like a tennis player spontaneously serving a ball

Like a ballerina completing an instinctive plié

A violinist uncontrollably swiping his bow

Passion

Ease

Fury

I needed no lessons

No teacher

No books

I climaxed with an euphoric subcutaneous orgasm

And kissed my emotionless lover in a bloody numb afterglow.

My God, the feelings you have when you are not connected to reality are intense. I did love James, but I love the feeling of not being alone tenfold. I was very sheltered growing up, I was protected, loved, and at the same time so overprotected that when bad things happened to me I was afraid to tell anyone. I held everything inside me. It didn't eat at me, like one would think, because until I met James I was so privileged, I didn't understand half of what was wrong with my childhood. I didn't know bad was bad, until I was actively bad. James introduced me to a world of experiment, drugs, sex, and rock and roll, not to be cliché, but all those things Catholic school doesn't want you knowing about.

I wish Catholic school, my parents, my friends, someone would have TOLD me, TALKED to me, EDUCATED me about bad things. Instead of just setting them aside as sin, they should have let me know the EFFECTS they have, the serious psychological and emotional effects that drugs and sex can have on you. I probably know more about why not to listen to Helter Skelter – it's the devil you know? I knew to wear a condom because Linder Ellerbee told me too, but then my mom changed the station when she began to put it on a banana.

What I have learned about MY mental illness is that I equate sex with love. And love is everything. Love is a reason to live, being loved is a reason to wake up in the morning, receiving love is so great that I give it back too hard. It's like Tommy Boy and the bird; I tend to snap my partner's little neck off while petting it. I still wonder WHY love feels so good to me. I read once that people with Borderline Personality Disorder feel emotions uncontrollably. That's true, it's part of the reason I cut. In a psychotic state, watching the blood run out is like watching my emotion pour onto the floor and out of my heart.

And to the therapists who say cutting is bad - and believe me, I've been one of them - you have NO idea how good it really feels. And a therapist's concern, no matter how genuine, doesn't trump the feeling, the emotion of love. It also doesn't make me feel better about being abandoned, which is like a sinking, sick, scary, heart-wrenching, short-of-breath, on-going never-ending, feeling. And nothing anyone does can change it, take it away, or fix it. You have to adjust to it. It's only a feeling. It's not life. I have had to learn that my emotions are not my life. They are two separate things that control each other, and I learned how to control both separately.

I did love James, but not in a healthy way. I later used my experience to talk to teens about healthy relationships. After all, I knew unhealthy. James was psychologically abusive, verbally abusive, and at one point physically abusive, but I was sick and didn't know it. I was so ill, and the amount of hell we put each other through was equal.

Jaden Christopher

March 2002

Dear James,

You lacked so much love for me. How could you disrespect another person the way you did? You have raped my soul, and my mind - I don't know where to turn. I broke underneath you, turning into an insanity-ridden delinquent. I followed you wherever you went, I don't know why. You weren't good for me. Unable pick myself up after you betrayed me. I am unable to do anything but go to a psychiatrist and sit in an amitriptyline coma. The whole time blaming you because I couldn't have you; never blaming myself or my own mental illness; the doctors didn't even blame that.

You tricked me into returning to you, and I was so vulnerable, so immature, so lost and so alone. It was all new to me; I wanted to experience your world - your sin, while I was numb enough not to feel guilt for doing so. Everyone says I am a stupid little girl. They are right; you call me names, you degrade me, you continue to betray me and yet I stay.

Attempting to own a life that isn't mine, leaving my comfort zone in an attempt to impress you, and leaving my life behind as a Catholic school girl Prom Queen.

~Hell Has Pulled Me In~

Jaden Christopher

Clique Clack

I am marching with military girls
Left foot – right foot – Glitter boots
Don't fit the sounds – get my noose
Click – clack – clique – clack

Daddy's money pays your bills – pays for pills
Covered in sin and covered in black
Traitor to the Nazis of cocaine and crack
Click – clack – clique – clack

Cut it up with my nine inch nails – cannot fail
Little pills to solve my woes
One quick snort and here I go
Click – clack – clique – clack

Blood and bile – downward spiral
Heart's still beating
Wrists are bleeding
Click – clack – clique – clack

Little cuts – little sorrows
Scars I'll have until tomorrow.

A Toast to French Roast

You coffee shop bastard
Burn your tongue
Choke on the mocha
That flavors your tales

I sneak
Slowly behind you
Into your dreams
Into your brain
I seep hot liquid into your veins

Drip drop
As the blood seeps from my cuts
Drip drop
Black like the burnt liquid in the bottom of the pot

Pastry?
Cake?
Apparently you can have both
And eat them too

Sleep next to me
Whisper in my ear
Of your coffee shop tales

The girl behind the counter
Rings up your bill
My money paid the tab

Red bricks
Painted with your eye on them
I have my eye on you

Jaden Christopher

Always

I know

And yet

I stay.

Village of Lies

Pride in Failure
Hanging on the fridge

Forgotten family
And a life before you
Unknown, lost

One touch
Happiness
One line
But not with a pen

Unnecessary
Accomplishment
Made us closer
Lack thereof
You loved my sin

Loved my failure
Loved my fall
Fast it was
Till I was on your level

Love as a drug
Masochistic addiction
Consumed
By the devil

Dirty and wrong
A martyr
For every Catholic school girl
But a girl and that's all

Jaden Christopher

Nothing Special
Never again
I'm in love with my sadness
You're in love with a borderline.

April 2002

Dear Doctor,

This is my Slit Wrist Theory: I think we all want to be delivered from the hell of our personal reality, and sometimes we wake up for a brief moment to realize we can no longer feel, sometimes we wake up only to feel. Love creates such sorrow in all of our hearts, even when we are with someone who we care about more than ever, we can only be in agony until the second they come back; even if he has only left to go down the street for a pack of cigarettes. I await the moment when I let myself wake up and feel a spectrum of emotions, because right now all I can feel is the pain of heartbreak. The pain of loss overwhelms me, and therefore I cut.

I cut to feel something else besides what's ripping at my heart. The deep sense of drowning beneath your own covers while you lie in bed crying. Dreaming of the face you will never kiss again, of looking into the eyes you will never see again. We miss the feeling of love so much that we have no idea what it will be like to feel anything again. Those who are not afflicted by Borderline Personality Disorder can understand that reality is close by and someone else will soon come and bring them back to it. Some cut believing that maybe they will die, but most don't. I won't lie; I have cut for sympathy, as do many others. Sometimes I cut just to watch it bleed, as if the pain is escaping through the blood dripping from my veins, but it doesn't.

I feel no better after I cut than I did before. I still feel depressed and lonely, but more time has passed; I have managed to waste more of my life concentrating on where to cut so I don't die, yet bleed enough and cut deep enough to leave a scar.

I need to be hidden from all reality, sheltered from society because I don't fit in here. I want nothing more than to be a normal person, but it is never going to happen. I see all I used to be and I wonder how I got this far, this low. It makes no sense. I never should have left the city, I never should have started a relationship, I never should have dropped my life to be with someone who never really loved me.

I'm sick of the lonely apartment with my only friend being the computer. The repetitive browsing of internet pages, repetitive smoking of cigarettes, the go-to-work, go-to-the-mall rut… therefore I cut.

~Lost~

Amitriptyline Dream

Belle of the ball spinning so fast she loses herself
Dizzy and tired she falls asunder
Catatonic Prom Queen
Forever lost in her amitriptyline dream

Glass casket for all of St. John to see
Fairy dust and apples
What can set her free?

In the house of the seven dwarfs
Who whistle but don't work
Rice on the floor
Farewell to the Romanian Gypsy

Age 15 and 19;
14 and 30
Crammed in Raw
Like Eddie Murphy

Squirmy is the squire in his bottle on the fridge
My stoic king will kindly greet you
And after some whisky he'll kindly beat you

One day my white knight will arrive with Rapunzel locks
And with one kiss
Upon the Conneaut docks

Awaken this queen
From her amitriptyline dream.

Jaden Christopher

May 2002

Dear Doctor,

I love him more than I love myself. That is the problem. It always has been. Is it a crime to fight with the one you love? I don't understand how a relationship works. I lock myself in my bedroom night after night, fearing he will leave me if I move into his space. His space! Makes me laugh; I am paying the rent, I am cleaning the house, I have the car, it is my computer… but it is his space. He will leave me if I interrupt him at his computer. He is hiding something from me. So many questions, no wonder I am paranoid; I am tip-toeing around my own house, afraid to touch my own boyfriend.

I wait for him to come to bed, secretly lying awake until 3am just so I can feel the comfort I so desire. The warm hands wrapping around me or the solid heartbeat that came from his chest, for all of this I will wait; it is my time then.

He always kept me waiting for the day of his departure because I crossed the line of intimacy.

I made him hate me, I know I did. The names I can stand; the hand raising I can stand; the endless nights of crying I can bear, if only he will stay. He can't leave me, not now, not ever. On the outside I am fine; I talk of him with amazing devotion, a true love. And I love him, but I want it to seem special to everyone, I want them to think he is a passable guy. They do. Everyone sees us happy, playing together, sitting together, and having a happy home. Normalcy is the key. And never do we stray from it.

No one knows about the nightly ritual of separation. No one knows about the threat of abandonment. But everyone knows I love him.

~Confused by This Nightly Ritual~

Bathtub Romance

What's it been?
Over 2 years
I remember when John lifted this album for me from Sam Goody

I remember the first night in The Village of Lies

Popping it into the Playstation
Popping the pill into my mouth...

The bathroom with the sink outside
Sandalwood candles lit
From my alter to a nonexistent God
That I dearly worshipped at the time

I ran a bath
I sat there for hours
Naked
High
Dimly lit

Waiting, with the door closed
Waiting for you to come home

Naked
Sexy
Dripping with bubble bath

I sat and waited for hours
The candles melted
The CD played over
And over again
The water became cold

Soon I was shaking in the tub
Crying
Still high
But scared

I remember her voice
As she came through the door
With you
Would she find me?

Like a little girl
Who'd found her Christmas presents
Excited with the thought
Tears streaming down my face
The room was spinning
I was naked

Cold
Crying in the tub…
I stifled myself

Until you kissed her goodnight
And she walked out the door

As I walked the dark hallway
To our bed
In the dining room
I could smell her
Sweet sweat and sex

I could see you smiling because of her
Popped another pill
And fell asleep praying
You would touch me
I was unwanted
Unnecessary
Wasted.

Collar

40 ounces of drink
Dripping down my throat
One cool drop of bubbly liquid after another
Wakes up your memory
From across the room
I see you kiss her neck
Lick the collar I once wore on mine
Liquid numbness
Pig-nosed Bitch
Kisses you
Whispers
Goodbye, Goodnight

Right in front of me?
No
Right in front of you

Seduction as the door closes
First time
All over again
Kisses my neck
Where the collar used to be
We're both bitches now.

Village of Lies

Pounding
On the door, a dark stranger in this village of lies
Pretty
On this speckled counter, a foreigner to my cells
Donuts and coffee are pulling up for their night-time
tricks

As I suck on my Sippy cup
I lose myself amid the pool table
8 ball corner pocket, and my pole slides down the rob
zombie CD
A dollar bill unraveling, no purchase necessary for
tonight's ride

Choke on the dust from which this phoenix should rise
When will I be saved?
Save yourself little girl

Voices
From the hallway of my past
Question my actions
Hypocrites!
Hallucinations

Pluck the strings of my exhausted guitar
Play me
Until I bleed and callous and bleed again
Scar tissue is not a stranger to these cells.

Jaden Christopher

June 2002

Dear James,

There it was, hanging in the hallway closet; left the door open on purpose. May 10$^{th.}$ Prom. Really made me think, just the year prior I was the Prom Queen. Now I was sitting in the ghetto, snorting meth, sleeping in jeans and eating pills. He left the door open on purpose. I didn't touch it, didn't go near it, just sat there for hours listening to Alanis Morissette and staring at it. It was purple, should have been red. At least I knew on Prom night he would come home and sleep next to me, not her. Fiddled with the scars on my wrist... I lied to my therapist. Why did I love him so much?

Later that night, I remember a man showing up at our door. The cops were there and he was full of pills, and giving them away so he wouldn't get caught. The pill was large and white, it smashed easily on the speckled counter next to the stove, so easily it went up, up, up into my brain. I never knew what it was.

I didn't even know who I was, I remember sitting in Depot's room sporadically poking at the red bass as he loaded the rob zombie CD with clean white powder, I remember you saying, "You don't need a bump, play with the big boys, I'll draw you a line." I remember sitting there shaking from the pill I had already snorted, I remember rolling up that dollar bill. Oddly enough, there was never any money for food, but always enough money when you need to put a dollar up your nose.

You told me nothing would happen, it wouldn't hurt me. I pumped that line up my nose so fast and furious I didn't know what hit me. I was bleeding and coughing into your chest. "You can handle it, grow up little girl." I fell to the floor coughing, my heart racing, I didn't know what to do, it was more of a panic attack than the drugs, it was more of a scared thing. I was always scared... there was nothing in my life. I was out there on my own, I sacrificed my family to be with him, I sacrificed myself and my life to follow him around and be told to grow up. I lost... everything.

~Jaded Jaden~

Drugs

How can such an emotional thing
Be caused and called a drugged-out fling?
Touching made better by the cocaine
We loved each other, didn't know our own names
Crystal meth and nights of infatuation
Mornings of confusion and days of abomination
Drinking to death
Fucking on meth
Loving every second until consciousness set in
The liquor made you love me, and set us on a spin
Out of control, we were revolving around
And when our world crashed it made a riotous sound
We awakened to find our bed filled with blow
Couldn't believe we had sunk so low.

When James and I moved out of the Village of Lies we moved into a much higher ranking field of drugs, the Basement in the House of Mad. As I look back on this experience, even today, I am terrified. It was the first time I experimented with Ecstasy, and the first time I realized my drug use was a problem. I was pseudo-Wiccan, practicing black magic, vengeful spells, love spells, and drinking blood.

James and I spoke of returning to Chicago so I could go back to school at Loyola; I even bought two plane tickets for us to go apartment-hunting and to a college interview. That morning, I arrived at the House of Mad and James was drunk, lying on the floor in the basement, throwing things at me and screaming. He got into the car and almost jumped out half way down the street. I turned around and dropped him off back at the house, got on the plane and went and wandered round Chicago that day by myself. I came home the same night. I was out of my mind, thinking I could go back to school, and to this day I am embarrassed at how I must have presented myself to the interviewer.

At the House of Mad James became an Oxycontin addict. He bought them in large quantities from an AIDS patient who they were prescribed for and didn't use. He also began a methamphetamine lab in the basement. Shortly thereafter, I moved out and got my first apartment, all by myself. James moved in weeks later.

Recalling that time in my life, I think of the numerous antidepressants I was taking; no mood stabilizers, no antipsychotics, and still taking eight Triavil and eight Atarax daily. I was so manic it was unreal. I can barely remember most of it, but I do remember that my apartment walls were covered in old records, sheets, and my poems. I was very proud of my poetry. I also utilized old lingerie for curtains. My grandparents came to visit me there. That's sad. It's sad to think my grandfather died shortly after my real recovery began, and that he had to see his little granddaughter so messed up, so sick, and so helpless.

My grandparents were always my rock. My mother is now, but we were at great odds when I was first getting sick. My grandparents stood by me, no matter what I did or what went wrong. Always understanding, always loving, always caring, and probably always just wanting the little girl they knew back. I'm glad I can give that to them now, even if my grandfather is in heaven watching it from there.

November 2002

Dear James,

You asked me if I wanted to roll as I was begging for something to get my mind off things. I said yes to the Blair Witch Ecstasy. I took that brown spotted pill and stared at it, I guess I could die. I mean, there is always a chance. The more I thought about it, the more inviting it became. Opened my mouth, downed some Gatorade… two minutes later… it's not working, I'm too used to snorting… five… nothing… ten… nada… fifteen… the brown couch was pretty soft… twenty, and I'm dry humping the shag carpeting.

As I lay there running my hand through the dirty brown carpet that hadn't been swept in years, I was in heaven. The touch, the strands individually going through my fingers, wrapping themselves around my skin, flicking my nails on the root, damn, this was some good carpet.

I recall some people coming by to buy some drugs; they inquired about me, I'll take what's she's on they said. I felt absolutely wonderful; this beats manic euphoria any day. And it's the first time I have felt better than OK in a long time. I was the world's best salesman that night.

The sounds of Billie Holiday blared on the stereo, as silver tinsel dripped into my face, and then we blew up. I lay back into your arms, Juan grabbed one of my legs,

Craig my other. Ashley on my right arm and Sara to my left and Mad straddling me with glow sticks and Vicks vapor inhaler, blowing it into my mouth, nose, eyes, all over my face. Juan and Craig rubbed my legs down, Ashley and Sara my arms. Every sense of me was awake and yet so drugged, every centimeter of my body was full of feeling. All of a sudden you started rolling my head around in circles and Mad took a big puff of Vicks and blew so hard I felt God himself on my face. Mad yelled "stop", everyone dropped me, you let my head fling back, and nothingness rushed over me.

For that moment there was no world, no hell, no heaven, no fear, no tension, no mental illness, no you, nothing.

~Relieved and Sane~

Sugar High

Red Hot Devil Whore
Syphilis of the brain
Kept home on Prom night
Bleeding out the sickness
Strawberry Lattice scars

Laffy Taffy Noose
"Don't go near it"
"Don't even think about it"
Cocaine and Kiwi Psychosis
Asphyxiation in the doublewide

Amitriptyline Queen
Flat back on an Oxycontin candy carpet
Spinning in a room
High on button candy Vicodin
I lied to my therapist…
Said I was the Prom Queen…

I used to be?

Jaden Christopher

Dinner in the House of Mad

Black and Blue chicken thighs
Orgasmic sighs and bloodshot eyes
Up for days cooking meth
3 days straight on trucker's caffeine

Powdered sugar French toast sticks
Bailey's and cream and butcher block wrists
Mad Hatter tea parties with her static TV dinners
Flame grilled anger and factory shampoo

Strawberry fuckers and chicken heads
A meal in a pill and a breakdown
In the black hefty bag
Sudafed mints to hold you over

The Easter bunny on the front lawn
Busting eggs as we drove by
The basket was out of rolls
He turned you in

With his sugar coated jollies and edible ego
The Mad Hatter was pink slipped
Turkey tryptophan is gone
Haldol for breakfast, intramuscular dinner.

Fire trucks in the House of Mad

The basement in the house of mad
The smell of red Sudafed
And chemicals cooking in the next room

Dark grey
Damp
Concrete walls
The sheet-less mattress

Surrounded by empty dusty bookshelves
Her movie theatre cup of Mountain Dew
I remember
Laying awake at night
Waiting for you to wake up crying
Or screaming
I never knew why

There I was filthy, un-showered, and unclean
Tweaking out of my mind
Wide awake at 4am
We always slept in our clothes

I had escaped my horrible middle-class surroundings
And a mother
Who cared
And prayed
Every night that I would come home

…

At the age of 20
On Christmas morning
You awoke to find a shiny new fire truck

Jaden Christopher

With sirens gleaming
Red with fury
Waiting to save someone's life

You broke it immediately
Tore off the tires
So it couldn't drive away
Ran it under water
The pressure peeling away the paint

Used
Abused
Dim
So ugly
No one wanted to play with it

Yours
Only
Who else would want it?

No one would dare steal it from you now
You took out the batteries
It couldn't make a sound

Shout out for fear
Shout out for help
Or even tell you how much it hurt

...

You awoke screaming
I crawled out of this thought for a second
Stumbling up the stairs
To the stash box

Little white tin under the brown couch
Under Mad's sleeping lifeless body
I ran to that white powder

Amitriptyline Queen

The powder of life
That sprinkled itself across the heads of everyone in the house of mad

Pounded a bump
Dug for a pill
Something
Anything to take it all away
Escape

Flutter our eyes
Curl our toes
And dismiss you back to sleep

If you were silent
Then I could dream
Of days when that little red fire truck was on the store shelf

Box unbroken
Sirens blaring
Hope abound.

Jaden Christopher

September 2002

Dear James,

Do you remember sitting in Mad's basement with the strawberry fucker and the ex-con? You hit me... You slammed your fist into my thigh and laughed. The people around you were stunned; yes, the man who fucked girls and paid them with coke was stunned. You were drunk, had just finished off a fifth of whiskey. You didn't care, if only he had seen my legs under the jeans, if only he had seen my arms, my wrists. Granted, I did the wrists myself, but damn, it was due to you. No one knew, no one knew you like I knew you. I was damned around town for uttering a word of what you did, shunned from my peers, my school, my friends, you coked out son-of-bitch. I poured myself into the mould you made for me, and whatever didn't fit got smacked down.

God, how you cried the nights away with the "I'm sorry" and the "I love you"... how was I supposed to know??? They were so empty to you... and so full for me. I was in a cloud, I was walking above the world, because someone loved me, someone was interested in me... I have never felt more used after being with you. And I have never felt more confused while being with you.

~Unsafe~

All Too Well

I know myself all too well
So much so that I am afraid
Like waves of an orgasm washing over my body
My feared Self is released
First into my mind
Then through my actions
The chain smoker
Afraid to open her doors
Sitting content in a cold dark room
With a razor running up her arm
Actual Self
Paralyzed by the constant headache
Of manic thoughts racing one past another
Flickering
Sick
Over how disappointed the world will be
Because I needed a break from reality.

In February 2003, I began taking Depakote and my world changed. So did my waistline. I broke my ankle in May of 2003 and my mother moved me out of the apartment, away from James, away from drugs, and into recovery at her house. I had to take meds, I wanted to take meds. I was so consumed at this point by my mental illness that I couldn't escape it. And although I had been seeing psychiatrists for 2 years at this point, no one ever gave what I had a name. No one ever said Bi-polar, Borderline Personality Disorder. It was like my diagnosis was a secret. No one ever talked to me about self-medicating (drug use to manage mental health symptoms) no one ever said I could have a chance of escaping the life I was leading. If I didn't want to die because of depression; but let me tell you, I wanted to die because no one gave me the hope that there was an out.

Once I had found out my actual diagnosis in June of 2003, I wanted to read everything I could about it. That same summer I picked up the book Prozac Nation by Elizabeth Wurtzel. For the first time in my life I knew someone else had been there. She opened my eyes to mental health, and I could relate to her every word. I became a mental health investigator... reading everything, writing down my every thought, wanting to be like her, to help someone like she had helped me. I will never be able to explain what an impact Ms. Wurtzel and Prozac Nation had on my recovery, my art, and my writing.

Manic

Have you ever?
A game we used to play at parties
I always won

Have you ever
Felt so consumed by anger
You could kill someone?
Have you ever
Seen mutilated bodies
And thought they were yours?
Have you ever
Had a switch flip?
Have you ever
Been so sick and not known at all?
Have you ever
Wanted to die?
Because you thought it was beautiful?
Have you ever
Been Manic?

Jaden Christopher

Full Circle Rings

Naked
Dripping wet
Standing in front of the steamed up mirror
I stared at the metal bars that riddled my body
The scars that left road maps of my pain
Across my arms
The jet black hair that wasn't mine
An epiphany
Of who I was
I did not know this girl looking back at me
With a hardened face
In constant pain
Bloodshot eyes which used to be wide
Were now dimmed with the light of carnage
As I stood there
My face slowly deteriorated
I saw shadows of light
Moving across my peripherals
Ghosts of my past haunting me
I placed my hand against the glass mirror
And started to cry
Slowly I took them out
One ring at a time;
Eyebrow
Labret
Nipples
Tongue
Ears
Belly button
I cried for my natural beauty
The beauty that I had lost
In all his dark words.

March 2003

Dear Doctor,

Swish. Swish. Snort. Swish. Swish. Snort. It is when I am lying in bed next to him that I have my strongest homicidal urges. It's when he's fast asleep after a wonderful day together, after a night of amazing highs and never any lows. It's in that moment that I remember and recognize where I am. Reality sets in and I want to smother him with my socks, because I don't have a pillow to even sleep on. Maybe it's mania... not reality.

Awake in the middle of a dreary basement listening to him snore. There is never a thought of how his parents would feel. Who would he leave behind? No conscience. No remorse. No plan of what to do with the body.

I look over at that mountain dew movie theater cup and I know he's cheating, and I can't allow it, so I never leave his side. You call this co-dependency. I am dependent on nothing, I survive on nothing, it IS protection, survival in this game of post-teen relationships. It IS knowing that the second I leave, the asshole will call her to come over. And I refuse to let that happen. He calls it stalking, I call it relationship insurance. What the hell kind of relationship am I in?

Instead of counseling me on mental health and bipolar this and borderline that, you should tell me, just flat out tell me, that no one should have to live like this. Women… I… deserve better. That medication can't raise your self esteem or make situations go away. It is in a moment of clarity that you have taught me to reach for a pill, and whose fault is that? I am not dealing with delusion here. If you would allow me to focus on reality and just feel, for one damn second, how miserable I am then maybe I could figure a way out of this aside from smothering him or sedating myself.

Amitriptylizing the fact that I am miserable for a damn good reason is no way to practice medicine.

~Reality Killer~

July 2003

Dear Doctor,

A breakthrough! On this Independence Day I declare myself independent… of James… but what have I really done? Transferred my feelings you say, no you don't. Why don't you say this doctor? Can't be honest with me? Why don't you tell me I have just moved the James problems to Matthew?!? You appear to be fearful, or maybe lack insight. You should try ASKING what I am thinking, and not just commending me for finding someone better.

Still, on this day I stopped loving James as a savior and a saint. I no longer cared that he was truly a bastard. We hung out most of the afternoon, he told me he had slept with the camel backed girl - something I had assumed was going on for quite some time… one of the many, who cares? He told me I looked fat, I had gained weight. I thought "Of course I'm fat; I am taking Depakote by the gallon to make me feel normal."

I stumbled into his apartment with my crutches clutched to my side. I looked at him, and for the first time I saw him for who he really was. This Depakote… makes me fat as hell, but I can see.
My thoughts raced back to this picture I had seen on the internet; this guy with long blonde hair and a truly happy smile on his face. It occurred to me at that moment, I didn't want to be with James, I wanted whoever it was in that picture, someone who smiled and meant it. A

stranger. I was already in love with a stranger… Doctor, you should stop me now… and adjust my dosage.

James and I spoke for the first time since I had broken my leg. For the first time after I was diagnosed. For the first time, 3 months drug free. For the first time, 3 months on mood stabilizers and antipsychotics. I was being treated for my mental illness, for the crazy I had all along attributed to James. And now James becomes Matthew and I escalate crazy to the next level, bra.

My life becomes a metamorphosis, good for my future, horrible for the illness that will forever plague me until I take the steps to end the cycle.

Goodbye Depakote, Hello Abilify, but forever yours,

~Amitriptyline Queen~

Catholic Roots

Revelations
Final chapter
Deep breaths
I approached
The green door
On the corner of 49th and main
The rail of the stairs felt cold
Like holy water
White like the altar
And my once was savior
Stood at the top of them
Eye to eye
Slap me down
Words like sin
Say your penance
Enter the apartment
Enter your sanctuary
Smells of hamburger helper
And sex
With that camel backed girl
You confess
Cold steel crutches
Clutched to my side
Holding me up upon my broken leg
I stood strong
For 40 days I have fasted
Nothing of you
Thoughts raced back
To golden hair
With long waves of white in between
I no longer needed a savior
He was my angel
Unknown to me
Or him
My crutches tight to my side

I stood tall on my broken leg
Deep breath
One last fuck
I could see
You really were a bastard
Blasphemy
I rise above
And like Jesus on that 3rd day
Taken to my own heaven
Free
Of your hell

There were three guys in my life when I was with James, and they were the "band" and all I ever wanted from them was to not see me as a lunatic. To this day, I still think they do. James was a friend of theirs, and I had met them once prior to my psychotic break. James would never let me see them. He held the things that went on in a literally shit filled basement so secret. I would have to put out to listen to their music. One way in which he psychologically abused me. I wasn't allowed at their house, but found myself showing up only to find James not there, but out with another girl, and then crying in the front lawn with a drunken "Florida."

Florida was the guitarist, moved to my town from where else, Florida. He seemed sweet, we both liked to cut ourselves and drink lots of Vodka. The drummer was from Florida too, this sexy long blonde hair, but something was different about him. He has manners, morals, and is polite. He never said much to me, but let me bum a cigarette once and broke these drumsticks that James caught at a NIN concert. God, that was like the best thing I could have ever seen, because I knew how much James coveted those sticks. The bass player was cool, quiet, and nice and it was his house.

Three months into it… I was so in love. It was Halloween. I came home on the airplane from Chicago and James rode with my mom to pick me up. I had been talking about flowers, no one had bought me flower before. I thought that's what boyfriends were supposed to do. I went to his friend's house but I wasn't allowed in, not by the friend, but by James. It was almost as if he didn't want me to meet them. Was he embarrassed of me? Put your paranoia aside.

I walked up to this blue house and stood on the cement steps; it was the "band's" house. He helped them, I guess, with sound or something, I didn't really care. The house was dirty, kinda weird. There were Catholic pictures on the wall and an upright piano. This guy answered the door and asked who I was looking for, I guess there were a lot of people there James came up the stairs with a potted plant, orange, like what you would buy at K-Mart around Halloween time. The bass player looked at this plant with a what-the-fuck expression, and then looked at how happy it made me… once again, same expression? I was elated; I threw my arms around James. But he still wouldn't let me in; the "band" was private. The guys in the band… my future was just down stairs: Drummer, Florida, and the Bass player I never knew then what a big part of my life they would be and how things would really become full circle. The "band" was his thing that was private, important, secret. It wasn't the only secret.

In the Village of Lies James had a burned CD with the band, and he talked about something called a Korg. His friend was over and they were "privately screening" the CD. He made me sit in the living room. I really wanted to hear it; now I was more than intrigued. He held the CD over my head both physically and literally. I knew what he wanted, but I hated having him control me like this. I listened to the CD like a band whore, only he wasn't in the band. The CD did kick some ass but I wasn't allowed to hear it again. He kept it locked up. It wasn't anything amazing, but it was a new sound. Too bad I associate feeling like a whore with it. What's with these guys? Why wouldn't he let me meet them?

Jaden Christopher

Lunatic Fringe

Lunacy in my Tommy Hilfiger dress
A band whore to a nobody computer nerd
Anyone can flick my strings
Jealous?

Breaking your sticks
Florida whisks back 105 Vodka
Like he knows my pain
Does it Burn?

Lend me your fire, pass that flame
Long blonde hair surfing those Florida waves

You are the toilet that these guys piss on
And I am the mop of the night-time cleaning crew

There's power in sleeping with the enemy
Had Enough?

I was with James for 2 years, but spent 6 years wishing I could redeem myself to these guys; all I ever wanted was for them to understand why... In August 2003 I met Matthew, the drummer's 30 year old brother, and being free of James, I was free to fall in love, and I did... hard, borderline hard.

Matthew and I had a relationship that began in July 2003 and continued through August 2006. He had just moved into town and it was a fresh start for both of us. This relationship was the key in my knowing I truly was ill. It was like nothing I had ever felt before; it was like walking above the clouds. I always thought I had known Matthew prior to us meeting, in a different life; we connected and bonded immediately. I was taken with him, his family, and his lifestyle. And all the while I was clingy and terrified of this possible abandonment by him. I acted in ways that I never should have, he described it as being "up his ass with a microscope" which was true. I could not lose him; however, it was my behaviors, this reaction to a fear of an unreal abandonment that led to the failure of the relationship. I acted out of total desperation when there was no need for it, and I got even more desperate when he left. I probably wrote a million emails begging him to take me back... why? Because Matthew was proud of me, he loved me, yes, but he took pride in having me on his arm, just for who I was. I will never forget this; the self esteem that was awarded to me through being in this relationship was overwhelming. He kept me clean, he kept me sober, he kept me happy, mildly euphoric, maybe hypo-manic, but happy. Most of all he allowed me to psychoanalyze myself, to become aware of my mood cycles, my borderline traits and love myself for who I truly was. He taught me to love myself, and by 2006 I was able to do that for a little while.

The break-up between Matthew and I was hard, it was abrupt and unexpected on my end. Although I was terrified of abandonment, I never thought it would actually happen. But again with that Tommy Boy bird, if you squeeze something too hard its little head will pop off... I wish Matthew would have ended things differently with me, not over the phone, not so suddenly... but sometimes you have to pull a borderline off like a Band-Aid. I have come to the realization that he couldn't have escaped any other way.

There were so many good parts of this relationship that it's difficult to write them all down, especially since it's so easy to see just the bad post-demise. But I truly loved him, he truly loved me. Abilify helped, Atarax helped, amitriptyline helped, I slit my wrists and did some drugs... that helped too. But most of all, I learned never to fall in love again. I was mentally ill, I was hard to handle, I came with baggage... no one would want me and I didn't want anyone who was going to only love an ideal hypo-manic Jaden.

July 27, 2003

Dear Matthew,

From the moment we sat face to face on the picnic table at Lake Shore Park, July 27th, 2003, I knew. I could see my future in your eyes, and it was good. I was hopeful; you made me want to know what was out there for me. I looked into those blue eyes and saw years of hurt. You checked me out, tried to figure me out, I was terrified of what you would find. Yet, you saw everything, and fell in love with me still. Everything in you besieged me. Your soul was beautiful and it knew mine. The moment we connected felt like I had known you for a lifetime. Save me! Fix me! Teach me! Love me! You were going to do everything no one ever could!

Sorry I set you up for failure.

~Mama Bear~

Jaden Christopher

August 2003

Dear Matthew,

I love you, I miss you, I adore you, and every second I am not with you I am thinking about you. I have never been more passionate about anyone before… in bed, in conversation and in love. For me, every day is like the first day we met; the butterflies in my stomach, the hot steamy kisses, and wanting to be the most beautiful girl in the room for you. Only everyday my love for you grows deeper, stronger and more everlasting. I have so quickly matured from a simple crush into an emotionally charged unconditional bond with you. I truly do feel like your soul mate.

To me you are the most beautiful person God has created, both inside and out. I thank him every day for sending me an angel like you to love and care for me. More importantly just for giving someone so contented to receive my love in return.

Sometimes I feel we can relate to each other without even talking. Just being with you calms and sooths me in ways no one could understand. It makes me feel loved. Safe. It creates an aura of happiness around me. A simple touch with no words spoken says so much to me. When I am not with you I feel lonely and I honestly think the void that has been in me all these years was "Matthew-shaped" because you are the one who fills it up completely.

Sweetie, I just wanted to say how much I love you and how much you mean to me, because after last night, I really realized that even your pure presence aids me in my daily life so much.

~A Princess Once Again~

Boomerang Illness

A delusion of grandeur in a deprived psychotic's world

The perfect escape plan for a bipolar borderline

Spontaneous isolation rouses thoughts of mutilated bodies

Awakens the manic depressive from her 15 minute slumber

And the pain comes flooding back; I just want to be numb

I didn't slit my wrists this time; isn't that enough?

But I still want to; I still plan to; I am going to…

Goddamn those forehead kisses

The rapid pressured speech of a mixed mood state

Flat effect from the queen's crown down

Sick wet vomit, voiding this agony from my body

I can't make out your memory from their voices; bastard? Cheater? Whore?

You're not sick; I'm not sick; I trust you…

I need some intramuscular assistance please

Abandonment triggers my boomerang illness

The sober alcoholic returns to the House of Mad

Kindling for the fire; burn me at the stake

Retreat and revive; I should have signed a DNR

Dyskinesia of the heart, the illness, the lifestyle

Get me out of this amitriptyline nightmare.

Jaden Christopher

August 18th, 2006

Dear Matthew,

Denial: No. No we are not. This isn't happening. This is wrong. You'll change your mind, I'll just let you cool off.

Anger: You fucking son-of-a-bitch bastard! Why would you tell me you love me so much 2 days ago and then cut off 3 years in one phone call? You bastard!

Bargaining: Dear God please, please, please don't take him from me. I'll give you anything. Dear Devil, don't let him go, I'll give you anything.

Sadness: I'm going to die, I want to die. Let it all stop. I need to slit my wrists; I'm going to slit my wrists. Please numbness, come over me…

Acceptance is yet to come.

~Grief Stricken~

Impeached

Outcast apple from an American pie
Fly that red, white and blue
You turn to the right, following Whitman
You swing inside like Ohio
Where's my faulty election?
Why did Florida desert me?

Was my campaign not strong enough?
Did I forget?
My morals
My values
My stance

I know I played dirty
Wore the wrong tie
In every debate
Bleeding heart

Impeached on August 18, 2006
With one phone call.

Jaden Christopher

Styrofoam Love

Map out our dreams on the lid of a generic white take-out box

You draw yours, I'll draw mine and we will blend them into doggy-bag harmony

The check comes and you're still drawing, Van Halen symbols of a life led

Before me

With me

After me

You do not sway from who you are, and yet your soul so strongly connects to mine

My beaver teeth, your bullet jean jacket, Daffy Duck and tiny thumbs

So much of our lives drawn out on a non-compostable map of the American dream

Before me

With me

After me

You're reveries which never transform but are recycled with lustful adoration

Until you find that faultless love: romantic, idealistic, and unconditional

And I will respectfully receive the consolation prize

A disintegrable utopia of what was our Styrofoam love.

Jaden Christopher

Catching a Glance

I still look for you
My eyes explore the crowds to catch a glimpse of your hair
Swinging above your brows, brushed to the side
No matter where
I grieve for your eyes
Blue as ice which now masks my heart
Once so in love with love
I dash from it
Once so in love with you
I thrust it aside
Catch me running
Throw your arms around me
Kiss me
Hold me
Love me
Once again
Maybe you remember me
Who I was before this emptiness
Remind me
I dream sometimes
That I am sleeping next to you
I pretend
Pretend
You long for me
Five minutes
Of how it used to be
Ten minutes
Touching you
I still glance for you in my heart, but memory is insignificant
I uncover you in my dreams, but fantasy is unresponsive
Reality is malicious
Find me in another sphere
I gave up on love
Don't give up on me.

Little Lollipop Girl

20 years old and an unknown soldier in an army of
Catholics
Judas was a bastard, how was she supposed to know?
Naïve little girl, what's an orgasm?
20 years young lollipop in hand and little plaid skirt
Black eye and slit wrists called her a borderline
Lack of identity and blood the DSM criteria
Knife in hand five years later
He's gone forever?
Memories flooding a chronic delusion
They call her a bipolar
Little male symptoms
She's a sociopath
You don't know the definition?
Worthless.

Dear Doctor,

A second time around: Why do I always idealize them? Why won't the abandonment fear subside? Why, after all the medications and the therapy do I still want to die when someone leaves me?

This anger, this resentment that builds inside me, is too much to swallow. Give me a pill for psychosis. Give me a pill for sadness. Give me a pill to help me start over. Better yet, just numb me up with your amitriptyline Novocain. Yeah... that hits the spot.

Now I can tell you all the answers.

My father left when I was seven. My mother never dated, and frankly appeared fearful of men. Someone abused me when I was four. My father stifled my crying with the phrase "I'll beat you till you bleed." I was left alone in the house at age three and woke up with no one there. I was teased all through school for being fat. I was laughed at during lunch while I ate, so I stopped eating during lunch. I hate men. I am afraid of intimacy. I went through a gauntlet of 20 adult men at age 13, then got beat up at school the next day. I am pretty sure my being voted Prom Queen was a big joke, like in the movie Carrie. No one ever wanted to date me. I hate myself and often wish I was dead. I was forced to watch porn at age 8. I used to hide in the car from my karate instructor.

I was always looking for an out, someone to take me away from my life.

A man… a knife, what's the difference?

Now tell me doctor… do you really care? You can't fix this with medication. You can't fix this with therapy. Tell me doctor… would you even remember what I just said if you hadn't scribbled it on your yellow legal pad? Tell me doctor… do you even know my name without your chart in front of you? Tell me doctor… if I kill myself today, how much does your malpractice insurance rise?

Here I go again, same pattern, empty threats. The truth is that I am scared… mostly of myself.

~Heart Broken a Second Time~

Jaden Christopher

Sick

I quit smoking
But
Stale cigarette smoke dances in the air
Jewel brings me back
My face flushed red
Hot
My stomach sick
From writing for hours
I remember you
How difficult it would be to write about
You
How difficult it would be to tell
Our Story
To remember the good times
In the shadows of distance
Quick sharp glimpses of our past
.gif files
Make me ill
Where are you now?
Where's my angel now?
I feel the vomit rising
Thinking sinking thoughts of our times
Happy cabin
Thrust me down on the bed
Smell of the sheets, periwinkle blue
I never liked you, snitzle
Greasy
Fried
I lied
Halloween baskets
Ripping the guts out
Forcing a face into their flesh
Coerced smiles
You worth light 100's
Scattered on the table

The Duke and Duchess of Ashtabula
Their kingdom has fallen
What are they worth now?
Nothing
But suppressed memories
And moments of sickness
When they bare their beautiful façade.

Jaden Christopher

Identity

Who I am is not what you've seen
Mothering Italian with her mommy's genes
Case consults and documentation
Days filled with abomination

Ambivalence was the status quo
Who was she without the woe?
In love with her sadness
Until she found bliss

Abandonment
Short love stint
Why did you? Did you?
It was the only thing she knew

Awakening now to find herself
Time to put love back on the shelf
Wasted and worthless she rides into the West coast sunset
Forever herself, forever regret

Love lost
Identity at great cost.

After Matthew I swore I would never fall in love again, and then after two years of celibacy I met Prospero. I had moved 3300 miles away from my home town in order to escape any possibility of seeing Matthew again. I was terrified to see him, to catch a glimpse of him, to continue on with my life in such misery.

When I moved I stayed with a friend and soon got my own place. I ran across a personal ad one day for Prospero. As I usually go by the pseudo name Ophelia I found this mildly amusing and worth investigating.

I met Prospero on April 12, 2008. Today we are still together and he supports me in all my efforts as a human being. He supports this book, my mental illness, my work and advocacy. He understands what happens when I don't take my medication and instead of just running away he reminds me nightly to take my pills. I love him, but not in a borderline way, just regular, regulated love.

I have worked for 8 years in the mental health field, advocating and assisting others with mental illness. I do not disclose my illness, as it is not my place to receive pity from my clients, nor is it my place to give pity; I give empowerment through knowledge.

I remain stable, drug free, alcohol in moderation, and on medication; one medication - Abilify. I still take Atarax as needed, but rarely do I need them. I haven't cut myself in 2 years but everyday it's still a struggle not to cope in the wrong manner. I still write, which has always been my most cathartic coping mechanism. I still talk with James and Matthew and consider them close friends. Prospero is supportive of this, and I love him for his understanding.

This book barely discusses Prospero, but I have to give credit, he is my creative muse and without him this book would not have happened. He may not be the contents of it, but everyday our relationship thrives and survives because I have been able to sit down with my thoughts and self analyze.

The Devil's Rebirth

Crimson droplets of madness drip: drip: drip: down my
thin skinned wrists
Each pin-sized bead a false memory unleashed through
my dreams
A Jungian perspective; my leaking subconscious
loathing

Questions burning like the Crucifix on my skin; flesh into
blood
Rivers of prayer flood: flood: flood: the internal drowning
sin
The devil's revenge: the anti-Christ within

Ophelia's soliloquy to the cunning bastard son:
Softly spoken breath: breath: breath: words of
vengeance
Hyper-distillation: renewal of the altruistic essence.

Jaden Christopher

March 8th, 2010

Dear Prospero,

I love you very much. You accentuate my true abilities and therefore I am a stronger, sexier, and more intelligent woman. My life is richer than I could ever imagine. I cannot envision a life without you. Sometimes I feel like I can come home after a complete letdown of a day and you are there to love me and get me through tough times. I feel free to fail at anything with you by my side, because you provide me with stability and truly unconditional love.

I think about our future together a lot and I understand you do not want children, and I cannot promise that this is something I am willing to forgo, however, I know I could be completely blissful and satisfied if it were only the two of us forever and I think that is what matters most.

The contributions you have made to my daily life over the past two years have been insurmountable. Knowing every day I will be loved, feeling unconditionally loved, cared for, accepted, nurtured, empathized with, sympathized with, interested in, and respected. I feel like we have had a lot of challenges over the past two years and I think we have come very far, and I do believe that this is the most unwavering relationship I have ever been in since my dating life began at 18-years-old.

Sometimes I cannot merely tell you how much you mean to me, because at this point the words "I love you" do not even suffice. You've been a committed companion, my best friend, a wise teacher, a respected mentor, a sensitive partner, a passionate lover, a father to our furry children, a funny, silly, and side-splitting roommate. You have been a source of my passion and of so much pleasure over the past two years. We have developed a relationship that is filled with depth in so many realms. I have tried to give you my everything, and in return I have taken on roles that are true to my heart and were previously veiled - the adventurer, the explorer, the mother, the writer, the poet, the traveler, the lover of all things Prospero, you have cultivated a young soul and will continue to do so my entire life. Within me you have fostered passions, feelings, drives, enigmas, and instincts that I never knew were there.

Inside the walls of our home (whether in Seattle, Boston, or Mars) I have found true happiness and within our family - you, me, Lilly, Voltaire - true meaning and purpose. The way our lives ebb and flow and our interactions complement one another, be it every second or within our whole life narratives. Although in your memoirs I may only be a short chapter, I would hope I can be present in every sentence your heart writes.

I feel like our life together encompasses everything I will ever need, want, wish for in life, and this is in part what you have given me, my one true love.

I ask of you only a few things - continue to be true to yourself, fight for what you love, and never forget to tuck me in at night.

~Forever Yours~

Jaden Christopher

Seattle Forgiveness

Knees deep in gravel; bruises forming
Sneakers dirt-coated with the cinders left from winter

Hunched over; Seattle rains tears
Forgiveness for letting you escape me

Betrayal; two hearts became three
Innocent party to a delusional mind and psychotic heart

White knuckles clenched around your velvet red jacket
Hidden emotions; tucked away safe

Broken hearts are inevitable; without pain, love is meaningless
Knees deep in gravel; new cuts form

My wrists have healed; don't leave me
My colorblind heart can see your androgynous shades of grey

Soon, my eyes will open to a prism of light; spectrum of colors
My once black-and-white God will grant me an Atheist

Panic ruptures solid ground; as I beg for this forgiveness…

Dear Doctor,

Yesterday I sat across from you in a grey cushioned chair. Yesterday I listened to your advice with no one to advocate for me. I followed your rules and listened naïvely to how I should take the pills, yet no one tells me what they are for, and no one tells me why I need them, and no one says that they will work, and all I know is they hurt my stomach and give me headaches, and no one cares.

Today I sit with a vast knowledge, self taught, self read and self experimented. I am smarter than you ever thought I could be. I have mental illness and I have a functioning brain, despite the drug use and despite your cocktails of amitriptyline and Atarax and Depakote and Seroquel and Zyprexa. I am 100 lbs heavier and I smile with a light you have never seen before. Chances are, I have taken whatever you are about to prescribe. Chances are you've read about it but never felt it circulate in your veins and in your brain and digest in your stomach and change your thoughts.

Today I am a walking, living breathing lab rat who beat the maze of mental health. Today I survive on 2 pills a night, not 8 like you wanted me to. Today I triumph over this thing and today I sit next to John Doe and Jane Doe and I tell them what you never told me. I know what they are feeling, I know a text-book delusion from a real one, and I have experienced crazy and I love it and miss it but never want to go back. Today when I can lay out every symptom for my client, when they cannot steer their way through the confusion of telling you about racing thoughts and manic euphoria, I can. I can navigate the system, their system and yours.

Today when you d/c my patient off of Depakote and don't titrate it down because you merely forgot, I am here to correct you and you hate that. But I'd take a correction and an ego hit to prevent a seizure any day.

And today when you berate me for not having a medical degree, I can only remind you that I used to sit across from you in a grey cushioned chair and now I sit beside you in the leather one. And yet all this experience and the degrees mean nothing to you, doctor. I am still mentally ill and I am a nonentity in your world of power and pills, just like your patients.

~Advocate~

www.ingramcontent.com/pod-product-compliance
Ingram Content Group UK Ltd.
Pitfield, Milton Keynes, MK11 3LW, UK
UKHW041412180426
11947UKWH00007B/96